CARIBBEAN CAMERA

A JOURNEY THROUGH THE ISLANDS

Christmas 1996.

A wander through our beloved islands

Love always

Celia + Lee

xxxx

Photographs by

OLIVER BENN

•

Text by

LENNOX HONYCHURCH

M

CARIBBEAN

First published 1992

Published by THE MACMILLAN PRESS LTD
London and Basingstoke
Associated companies and representatives in Accra, Auckland, Delhi, Dublin, Gaborone, Hamburg, Harare, Hong Kong, Kuala Lumpur, Lagos, Manzini, Melbourne, Mexico City, Nairobi, New York, Singapore, Tokyo.

ISBN 0-333-56605-X

Designed by Charles Design Associates

Printed in Hong Kong

A catalogue record for this book is available from the British Library.

ACKNOWLEDGEMENTS

I would like to thank the following people and organisations, who were of great assistance when I was taking photographs for this book. They are listed in alphabetical order.

Jamaica

Admiralty Club Hotel, Port Antonio; Jennifer Blair; Carleen Chang; Jamaica Tourist Board and Pat Mitchell; Patricia Parke; Barbara Preston; Shaw Park Beach Hotel, Ocho Rios; Marcia Smith and the Apple Valley Guest House, Maggotty.

Puerto Rico

Puerto Rico Tourism Company, Ponce and Zulma Collazo; Pedro Rinaldi; Spicy Caribbee, San Juan; Mary Wood.

United States Virgin Islands

Jack and Priscilla Dodds of Club St Croix, Christiansted.

British Virgin Islands

Charles and Ginny Carey and The Moorings Yacht Charter Company, Road Town; Nina de Vries; Sonia Williams of Island Services, Road Town.

St Maarten

Reinier Heere (Shipwreck Shops).

Saba

Wilma Hassell.

St Kitts and Nevis

Bird Rock Hotel; Hermitage Plantation Hotel; Greg Pereira (Greg's Safaris); St Kitts and Nevis Tourist Board and Hilary Whatley.

Antigua

Hugh Bailey (Catamaran Club Hotel); Dana Nicholson (Nicholson's Yacht Charter).

French Islands

Roseleen Joseph; Guadeloupe Tourist Office, Pointe-à-Pitre.

Dominica

Dominica Tourist Board and Norma Rolle; Deborah Fontaine; Paradise Tours (Joseph O Campbell); Reigate Hall Hotel.

St Lucia

Choiseul Craft Centre; Marquis Plantation and Vincent Biscette; St Lucia Tourist Board.

Barbados

Barbados Tourist Board and Hugh Foster; Garrison Secondary School, Bridgetown; Archbishop Granville Williams; Heywoods Hotel; Jill Sheppard; Nick and Sally Thomas (Sunbury Plantation House).

St Vincent and Carriacou

Lavinia Gunn (Noah's Arkade, Kingstown); George Gordon; Carl McLawrence; St Vincent Tourist Board and Janet Woods.

Grenada

Jean Baptiste (Sea Change, St George's).

Trinidad and Tobago

Arnos Vale Hotel; Victor and Zeta Peterson; Jeremy Taylor.

I am also grateful to the Caribbean Tourism Organisation in London for their very useful advice and introductions.

CONTENTS

Cuba
Haiti
Dominican Republic
Jamaica
Puerto Rico
United States
Virgin Islands
British
Virgin Islands
St John
Virgin Gorda
Tortola
St Thomas
St Croix
St Maarten
Saba
St Kitts
Nevis
Antigua
Guadeloupe
Lesser Antilles
Dominica
Martinique
St Lucia
St Vincent
Barbados
Petit Martinique
Petit St Vincent
Carriacou
Grenada
Lesser Antilles
Tobago
Trinidad
Colombia
Venezuela

INTRODUCTION

'ECLECTIC' is perhaps the best single word we can use to describe this diverse community of islands which we call the Caribbean. It is a region of broad contrasts where many races, languages, nationalities and abstract influences are compressed into a string of islands less than 2 000 miles from one end to the other and with a recorded history spanning only 500 years. But the sources of our heritage originate from far beyond those boundaries of time and space. Our people draw their traditions from every corner of the globe, and the history of those who inhabited these islands before the arrival of Christopher Columbus goes back thousands of years.

And spread like a bright blanket over this framework of past material grandeur is the spirit of the inheritors whose ancestors arrived on the islands with nothing. Taking this strand and that, rejecting one, embellishing another, modern Caribbean man and woman have sewn together a dazzling masterpiece. These strands are spread across the pages of this book: The rocking hymns of the Gospel Hall, the choreography of a dance company, the locks of a Rastaman and the tidy school uniforms showing the deep respect for education as the key to social and political change in this century.

An abstract view of this region on a map of the world would liken the archipelago to the body of a giant iguana lizard. Its head, legs and torso form the large chunks of the Greater Antilles and the green chips of its scattered vertebrae are the Lesser Antilles, a curving tail which touches the coast of South America. This scaly chameleon-like creature basks in the warmth of the northern tropics, poised between two sub-continents and washed by the currents of an ocean which deposits the flotsam and jetsam of the world upon the ever changing rhythm of its body.

Words, colour, rhythm. This is the language of the carnival costume designer, of the calypsonian, the wayside preacher and the flamboyant politician. This is the imagery and the abstract nature of things Caribbean. And how does one catch it, compress it into a few words, tidy it up and present it as a comprehensive whole? Like the cameraman I must resort to the vignette — the quick episode caught in the moment of a clicked button to represent a people and a place. But like the carnival costume builder I need a thousand images, stitched like sequins on a meshed frame, to tell the whole story. And I need music to make the revellers of my story come alive; I need the rhythm of the drum and the exaggerated emotion of the preacher and the politician to give it power. For the story of our islands is a powerful story, a colourful and bloody one, laced with words of anguish and exultation which has moulded a diverse people. It is like a carnival band with many sections. No section is the same, yet all is one, dancing to the same music in the same direction. And Carnival is in many ways a manifestation of the Caribbean story. It is made up of other people's scraps; the flotsam and jetsam of other people's cultures which, like the costume builder, we have made into our own unique and intricate design.

A collection of photographs is perhaps the best way to capture the elements and essence of this design. Only by using a collage of images can we hold still the colourful pieces which give it life and the intricate details which have merged to form the whole story, so that, like the variegated patterns on the costume, these pictures enable us to share the Caribbean experience with others. The camera, in skilful, sensitive hands, can hold the moment of change in the shades of a sunset, the reflection of the turquoise sea, the message in the glance of a market vendor or the joy of a children's cricket match. Pages of descriptive prose may not capture the full strength of an old fortress overlooking sweeping fields of sugar cane or the exhilaration of wind filling the sails of a racing yacht. Yet these are all chips in the kaleidoscope of images which, when placed together, tell the saga of our islands.

Like the reflectors of a kaleidoscope, or indeed that of a camera, these many images play upon the twin mirrors of man and his environment. The influence of one upon the other is a strong thread which runs through the tapestry of Caribbean history as people arrived here and came to terms with the new landscape which confronted them over the horizon.

The question of who we are and what we call ourselves is not as simple as it seems when one considers that our region has three different names: the West Indies, the Caribbean and the Antilles. It was Columbus' mistake in 1492 which forced on us the title of West Indians. He had miscalculated the circumference of the world by some 7000 miles and he believed, and tried to convince others to believe that he had landed on the out-islands of Southeast Asia. Worse perhaps was that he christened the Mongolian descendants who lived on these islands 'Indians'; a misnomer which they are stuck with unto eternity.

In an effort to try to correct this, the islands were soon being called the 'West' Indies. Then mapmakers recalled the story of the mythical Atlantic island of Antilia and slapped 'Antilles' on their maps of the islands as well. By the end of the 17th century the southern islands were being called the Charibby Islands or the Caribbees after the Caribs who lived there, and within another hundred years the whole archipelago became known as the Caribbean. Today, the term 'West Indies' is going out of Vogue and 'Caribbean' is taking over. Even in the question of nomenclature we don't know quite where we stand.

Names of places and people tell a lot about the Caribbean. Between 1492 and 1504 Columbus changed the names of over one hundred places. In the Lesser Antilles, the mysterious islands of Waitukubuli, Hewanora, Karukera, Wadadli, Aiachi and Liamuiga became Dominica, St Lucia, Guadeloupe, Antigua, Marie Galante and St Christopher. In the Greater Antilles, Haiti, Jamaica and Cuba were among the only ones to retain something like their original pre-Columbian names. Enslaved West Africans had their names changed without question to the simplest European forms: Ned, Bessy, Belle, Tom, Hall. Others were rechristened according to their African port of embarkation: Bonney, Congo Joe, Goree. On emancipation, the adoption of surnames became necessary and these were chosen from the Bible or from the surnames of their former masters and, in the French Roman Catholic islands, from the wide assortment of saints' days.

The names given to plantations by their respective owners tell something of the mood with which the plantocracy approached their enterprise. Hope is a common sentiment and there is at least one Hope Estate on each island. But even more confidence is expressed in such names as Castle Comfort, Easy Hall, Mount Gay, Content, Felicity, Harmony Hall and Fancy. My favourite perhaps is Whim in St Croix. The sheer nonchalance of the word and the visions it conjures up, represents so much of the nature of the plantocracy in the middle of the 18th century, before the worries of war, trade and declining prices had begun to set in.

Similarly a cruise through groups of islands such as the Virgin Islands will make any sailor realize what splendid hideouts they provided for 16th-century pirates. Many of these corsairs, freebooters, sea dogs, buccaneers, privateers, call them what you will, have stamped their names upon the map of these island clusters. Sir Francis Drake's Channel, Blackbeard's Cave and Dead Man's Chest, Fallen Jerusalem, Rum Cay, Treasure Cay and Barracuda Swash give an idea of the roguish humour of those who frequented these bays and inlets.

Plants and animals on the islands have a delightful array of names which often vary from island to island. What one fish is called in Grenada will often not be the same name it is given in Nevis. And this is particularly true with fruit. As new plants were brought to the Caribbean new names were devised, so that today different islands will call the same fruit by different names. This makes it very confusing for island-hopping visitors. The French creole islanders christened the breadfruit the 'yampain' — yam bread. What the Jamaicans call an O'Thaiti apple, people down at the other end of the Caribbean call a pommecytere. What one set of islanders calls a chou-chou another calls a christophene. You say chenip, I say kenip and the Barbadians call it an ackee, which in Jamaica is something completely different. But this is a lesson in history too, because it all shows how isolated the islanders were from each other before the 20th century. This relationship between plants, man and his changing environment can by itself tell the story of our islands.

The archipelago stands on the curved edge of two opposing tectonic plates on the earth's crust, along a subduction zone where the Atlantic Plate is pushing itself beneath the Caribbean Plate. This is why the Lesser Antilles are a chain of islands, a line of volcanic cones above the sea formed as a result of this arc of weakness in the earth's crust. And they are still being formed. In the southern Grenadines at Kick-um-Jenny an island-to-be is now slowly making its way up towards the surface of the sea. Active volcanoes rumble on St Vincent and Guadeloupe. The ruins of St Pierre in Martinique stand as mute testimony to the eruption of Morne Pele in 1902. Sulphur springs boil on Montserrat, Dominica and St Lucia. The placid Grand Etang of Grenada sits within a classic crater. The unique island of Saba is composed of one single volcanic cone rising straight out of the sea.

In the Greater Antilles, layers of sediment and limestone which were forced upwards by plate tectonics and then moulded by wind and water have created the marvels of Jamaica's Blue Mountains and Cockpit Country and the caves of Puerto Rico. In contrast, Barbados, Marie Galante, Barbuda, Anguilla, Sombrero and Anegada form a limestone outer arc of islands made up of flat coral terraces. Trinidad, at the southern end of this chain, was once part of South America and lies near the mouth of one of the largest rivers on the sub-continent. Its network of tributaries draws water from deep in the heart of one of the richest rain forest areas of the world.

As islands, we are very much subject to the flow of ocean currents, the course of sea breezes and the powerful blast of hurricanes, and it was the flood waters of the Orinoco which provided us with the indigenous plants of our islands. The South Equatorial Current curves northwards to join the Caribbean Current off the mouth of the Orinoco and then sweeps up along and between the islands like water through the gills of a fish. In this way, the matted beds of forest debris from the banks of the Orinoco were driven along the chain of the Lesser Antilles bringing the seeds and spores and roots to our shores. Our position between the tropical and temperate zones of the American continent also means that we are in the path of the annual migration of birds from north to south and back again, which was another rich source of seed dispersal and still influences the diversity of our bird life.

Our first human settlers used this route as well. Various tribes, the Ciboney, Arawak and Carib, came from the Orinoco region thousands of years ago using the same currents which had brought the plants. Their rough dugout canoes were carved from trees which they also found growing on the islands. Today the Gommier tree is still used in Martinique, Dominica and St Lucia for the construction of dugout canoes. The Amerindians were able to utilise plants to which they had been accustomed on the banks of the great river, so that botanically these islands were, in a way, an extension of the Orinoco River delta out into the Atlantic.

The pre-Columbian people also transported plants to the islands from South America, particularly those on which they most depended. And none was more important than the cassava or manioc. This was their daily bread. The most common artifact found in our pre-Columbian archaeological sites is the large round cassava griddle used for baking the cassava flour and the tiny chips of jasper used on a board to grate the cassava tubers. Clay, stone and wooden effigies of their spirits, called *zemis* have a flat top where offerings of cassava were made.

Cassava was an element of contact between the Indians and the post-Columbian arrivals from Europe. Just as the Amerindians were brought here by the flow of the Orinoco, so too did the Europeans arrive due to the Trade Winds from the Canary Islands. There are records of trading in cassava in the logbooks of visiting ships. In St Kitts the provision of processed cassava to the early English and French settlers by the Caribs was a key to their survival during the difficult first years of colonisation.

It was an Amerindian plant, the tobacco, which became the first commercial crop grown by the European settlers and it was the Caribs who taught them the method of cultivation in St Kitts. When the introduction of sugar cane began to change the fortunes of the colonists in the 1650s, the growing demand for land led to intense pressure by the French and British for possession of the traditional Carib islands of the Lesser Antilles. The continuation of small scale tobacco and cotton cultivation may have enabled European yeoman farmers and Caribs to maintain a precarious coexistence, but the fortunes of sugar after 1650 led to the final assault on Carib lands and the eventual retreat of the Caribs to Dominica and St Vincent.

The environmental destruction which was unleashed on these islands by the sudden expansion of plantations for sugar was phenomenal. The clearing of over 80 per cent of the rainforest on Barbados and the islands north of Guadeloupe was effected between 1650 and the end of that century. Jamaica, Puerto Rico and the southern more precipitous Windward Islands were tougher going and thus survived better. But even so, the land-grabbing and the denuding of forests around the coastal areas and larger valleys was thorough. The introduction of coffee by the French in 1725 added to the problem by making demands on the wetter, higher and usually steeper lands of the interior.

With colonisation had come slavery and the forced transportation on a large scale of West Africans, who added another important component to the culture and ethnobotany of the region. They adapted Caribbean plants to traditional African uses and those few Caribs who remained on the islands transferred their forest lore to the Afro-creole inheritors of their knowledge. What emerged from this combination was an awareness of the best uses and properties of various forest woods for different components of house construction, boat building, drum and tambourine fabrication and food preparation utensils. The knowledge of the uses of medicinal herbs was also transferred and in many cases adapted by the Africans from their knowledge of African plants. In those islands which still had sizeable stands of virgin forest the West African descendants developed a detailed forest lore which assisted with their survival. This was doubly important for the bands of escaped slaves, the Maroons, who roamed across the central mountain forests of Jamaica and the Windward Islands.

Feeding the growing population of slaves on the islands became a major concern for the colonial administrators. The problems of existing trade restrictions and the war with the American colonies who were suppliers of the staple food, livestock and building materials for the islands, contributed to these pressures in the 18th century. At the same time a more scientific approach to exploration and tropical botany led to greater knowledge, experimentation and innovative uses for plants from other parts of the tropics. The story of the introduction of the breadfruit is one of the best examples of this link between administration, empire, exploration, transportation and economics with the fortunes of a particular plant.

INTRODUCTION

In 1772, Valentine Morris, Captain General of St Vincent wrote to botanist Joseph Banks in England about the possibility of introducing breadfruit to the British Caribbean Colonies. It took another 15 years for the project to get moving and for a ship, HMS *Bounty*, to set sail. Although the breadfruit story grabbed the headlines, many other food crops and spices — nutmegs, cinnamon, peppers, cloves and others — were being introduced here from Africa, Southeast Asia and the Pacific to add to our growing larder of exotics.

The collapse of the sugar industry on the English islands after the 1840s was due partly to the British Sugar Duties Act of 1846, which ended trade protectionism, and partly to the abolition of slavery in 1838 and the failure of British planters to modernise their equipment. Meanwhile, in the Spanish islands such as Puerto Rico, sugar entered a period of booming prosperity which blossomed in the architectural opulence of the southern city of Ponce. Today many of these buildings have been restored and are the pride of Puerto Rico.

While the British islands were searching for new crops to rebuild their collapsing economies, a new influx of people were entering the Caribbean. East Indian indentured labourers from the east coast of the Indian subcontinent were transported to the Caribbean to cultivate plantations, particularly in Trinidad and Guyana. They too brought their own religions and social, as well as ethnobotanical traditions.

It is at this time that we see the establishment of botanical gardens in Grenada, St Lucia and Dominica to join those in St Vincent and Jamaica, established over 100 years before. Besides the economic plants which were being introduced, the flower gardens of the Caribbean were being enhanced by the constant increase in the importation of flowering trees and shrubs from all corners of the tropics. The introduction of the hibiscus into Martinique and its regional dispersion from there is a case in point. Earlier, in the 18th century, Bougainville had introduced the bougainvillea from the Far East and a century before that the French governor, Du Poincy, had cultivated the Poinciana, or Flamboyant, in the Leeward Islands. By the dawn of the 20th century colonial commissioners had issued reports proposing the propagation and cultivation of cocoa, limes, bananas, coconuts and citrus which, along with sugar, became the cash crops of the modern Caribbean. Like the people, hardly any of the fruit now common in the islands are indigenous to the region.

Today, as we drift southwards from Jamaica along the Caribbean chain, each new sight and experience links together to form a coherent whole. A plantation greathouse, a ruined fort, a sing-song turn of phrase, the gaudy colours of a village dwelling, the vibrant sound of the tambourines at a prayer meeting and the repetitive roll of reggae all become part of the same story.

The pre-Columbian stone carvings in Grenada, the Taino Indian ball courts in Puerto Rico and the descendants of Caribs in Dominica, building their dugout canoes, are the traces which lead us to the first human settlements on these islands 5 000 years ago.

Along the cobbled streets of the old Spanish city of San Juan, Puerto Rico, we walk in the footsteps of the Iberian conquistadors. We climb over fortresses and enter old city gates where foundation stones were laid during the dawn of the Renaissance. Yet the activity which bustles in the streets around echoes with the brash vibrancy of United States influence in the modern Caribbean.

The Spanish language and customs still hold strong there but across at Port Royal in Jamaica we peer through the gun embrasures of Fort Charles from where English buccaneers sailed out to cripple Spanish power in the region and thus turn the tide of European influence in the islands. The small maritime nations swept across the Atlantic in a mad grab for new territories. As commerce prospered, the Netherlands occupied a number of islands to be used mainly as trading posts, to store and exchange goods and refit their ships. These Dutch colonies were quite small and included St Eustatius, Saba, St Maarten, Curaçao, Aruba and Bonaire. The descendants of these early settlers still cling to the hillsides of Saba, inhabiting neat whitewashed houses of distinctively Dutch character.

In the old town centre of Charlotte Amalie, St Thomas, we capture the influence of Danish colonial architecture where the Danes made their first Caribbean settlement before claiming St John and St Croix in the early 18th century. All three remained Danish until 1917, when the United States purchased the islands to keep them out of the hands of the Germans and with an eye towards the security of the newly opened Panama Canal.

French corsairs had been raiding the Spanish since 1506 but finally settled down to begin colonisation in St Kitts in the 1620s. From there they spread their possessions to Martinique, Guadeloupe and its dependencies, St Domingue (now Haiti) and, from time to time, Grenada, St Lucia and Dominica. The art galleries, restaurants and sidewalk cafés of Fort-de-France and Pointe-à-Pitre capture the Gallic milieu which has taken root in the tropics.

The fact that these were islands with the ocean as their connecting highway, gave the seafaring British the upper hand from the earliest days of colonial conflict. At Nelson's Dockyard, English Harbour, Antigua, and on the ramparts of Brimstone Hill Fortress, St Kitts, we see something of the powerful network of naval control which held each island colony together. In the cool shade of the plantation greathouses of Barbados, Jamaica, Nevis and St Kitts there is an uneasy calm as we reflect on the method of extracting the elegant fruits of that power.

Oliver Benn captures these aspects as well as the edifices which link our people to our heritage and each one of us to our own special island. The relaxed atmosphere of Virgin Gorda's Easter Festival; a beach barbecue at Morant Bay, Jamaica; tending bananas in St Lucia; fisherman pulling seine nets or women sorting nutmeg mace at Gouyave, Grenada. And it all climaxes with the spectacle of Carnival in Trinidad, like the last lap on the night of Shrove Tuesday, the wild culmination of a journey through these eclectic isles.

LENNOX HONYCHURCH

Jamaica

The Blue Mountains, seen from Port Antonio.

Devon House, a restored 19th-century mansion in Kingston. Built by a Jamaican who made a fortune in South America, it is now a museum furnished with antiques of the period.

Two of the island's 18th-century Great Houses, originally the hub of extensive sugar plantations.

Above:

In the living room at Brimmer Hall, near Port Maria.

Left:

The dining room at Greenwood, near Falmouth, built by the Barrett family (formerly of Wimpole Street).

A worship meeting at the Prayer Tower, one of the many independent sects which flourish in Kingston.

Above:

Members of the congregation at prayer

Right:

Sister Esmé, the Minister, is asking God to heal a sick child.

CAYMANAS PARK RACECOURSE, NEAR KINGSTON.
Left:
A TRAINER GIVES INSTRUCTIONS TO HIS JOCKEY.
Below:
IN THE GRANDSTAND DURING THE ENSUING RACE.

INFORMAL CRICKET PRACTICE NEAR PORT ANTONIO.

WEIGHING YAMS BEFORE SALE AT WAIT-A-BIT, A VILLAGE IN THE COCKPIT COUNTRY.

A Rastafarian in St William Grant Park, Kingston.

Another Rastaman with his roadside stall near Ocho Rios.

AFTER A SERVICE AT THE BETHESDA GOSPEL HALL, PORT ANTONIO.

A FAMILY WITH PART OF THEIR BANANA CROP, NEAR ALBERT TOWN IN THE COCKPIT COUNTRY.

IN THE ALL-AGE SCHOOL AT ACCOMPONG IN THE MAROON COUNTRY. DESCENDED FROM RUNAWAY SLAVES, THE MAROONS ARE A SELF-CONTAINED COMMUNITY WHO STILL LIVE IN SOME DEGREE OF ISOLATION.

THE YS FALLS, NEAR MAGGOTTY.

IN SHAW PARK GARDENS,
OCHO RIOS.

Rafting on the Rio Grande.

Catalaya orchids.

Hibiscus flowers.

Black-eyed Susan.

Rose Hall on the north coast, once the home of the notorious plantation owner, Annie Palmer.

PORT ROYAL, THE FORMER BUCCANEER CAPITAL NEAR KINGSTON.
Right:
BEHIND THE GUN EMPLACEMENTS IN FORT CHARLES.
Below:
THE GIDDY HOUSE ON ITS SUBSIDED FOUNDATIONS.

THE TWIN HARBOURS OF PORT ANTONI(

Dancer/acrobats performing at the Shaw Park Beach Hotel, Ocho Rios.

The Jamaica Dance Theatre Company, Kingston, at rehearsal.

Beach barbecue at Morant Bay, [s]outhwest coast: goat fish and [o]ther local delicacies are cooked [f]or lecturers and other staff of the [U]niversity of the West Indies.

SAN JUAN: WALLS OF THE OLD SPANISH CITY WITH THE SAN JUAN GATE AT THE RIGHT.

THE SPANISH CUSTOM OF WATCHING PASSERS-BY IN THE EVENINGS (PLAZUELA DE LA ROGOTIVA, SAN JUAN).

CALETA DE LAS MONJAS, SAN JUAN, WITH THE CATHEDRAL IN THE BACKGROUND.

DETAIL OF HOUSE FACADE IN CALLE FORTALEZA, SAN JUAN.

PARQUE DE BOMBAS, PONCE. THIS MOORISH-STYLE WOODEN BUILDING (1883) WAS, UNTIL 1989, THE HOME OF THE LOCAL FIRE STATION, AND IS IN CURIOUS JUXTAPOSITION WITH THE MUCH OLDER CATHEDRAL SEEN IN THE BACKGROUND.

PRIVATE HOUSE IN CALLE REINA, PONCE, WHICH ILLUSTRATES THE CITY'S CHARACTERISTIC MIX OF CLASSICAL AND OTHER ARCHITECTURAL STYLES.

STUDENTS DRESSED FOR A PROCESSION AT PENUELAS, NEAR PONCE.

SANTOS — SMALL WOODEN FIGURES OF SAINTS, CARVED AND PAINTED BY HAND — ARE A PUERTO RICAN SPECIALITY. THESE EXAMPLES ARE BY PEDRO RINALDI OF PONCE.

MIGUEL CARABALLO, A PROFESSIONAL MASK MAKER OF PONCE, WITH SOME OF HIS HAND-PAINTED PAPIER MACHÉ CARNIVAL MASKS.

A typical landscape in the island's centre, near Utuado.

Lago Caonillas in the same area

IN THE RAIN FOREST AT EL YUNQUE.

THE SINK HOLE IN THE CAVES AT RIO CAMUY.

THE RE-CREATED TAINO INDIAN VILLAGE NEAR PONCE — THE ORIGINAL SETTLEMENT FLOURISHED BETWEEN 1000 AND 1500 AD.

ONE OF THE BATEYS, OR COURTS, NEAR THE TAINO VILLAGE WHERE BALL GAMES WERE PLAYED. THE GAMES PROBABLY HELD SOME RELIGIOUS SIGNIFICANCE.

A COURTYARD OFF CALLE CRISTO, SAN JUA
THE BUILDING IN THE BACKGROUND WA
SUCCESSIVELY A BROTHEL, THE HOME OF TH
WELL-KNOWN LOCAL POET JOSE GAUTIER BENITE
AND NOW HOUSES A SHOP SPECIALISING I
LOCAL SPICE

SPICY
CARIBBEE

UNITED STATES

VIRGIN ISLANDS

ST THOMAS

THE BEACH AT MAGEN'S BAY.

DANISH COLONIAL ARCHITECTURE IN THE OLD TOWN CENTRE IN CHARLOTTE AMALIE:

Above:

MARK ST THOMAS INN.

Right:

TOWN HOUSE NOW USED AS LAWYERS' OFFICES.

Part of the 99 steps on Government Hill, Charlotte Amalie.

THE LEGISLATIVE BUILDING (1874), STILL THE MEETING PLACE OF THE UNITED STATES VIRGIN ISLANDS' SENATE.

THE GRAND HOTEL BUILDING (1843): PROBABLY THE EARLIEST MAJOR HOTEL IN THE CARIBBEAN.

St Croix

THE CHARACTERISTIC YELLOW PLASTERWORK OF OLD CHRISTIANSTED:
Left:
FORT CHRISTIANSVAERN.
Above:
PARLIAMENT BUILDING.

ONE OF THE TWO PUTTI, PROBABLY 18TH CENTURY, ON EACH SIDE OF THE WHIM GREAT HOUSE ENTRANCE.

THE ANIMAL-DRIVEN MILL IN THE GROUNDS OF THE WHIM GREAT HOUSE, ORIGINALLY USED FOR SUGAR PRODUCTION, WITH THE WINDMILL WHICH REPLACED IT IN THE BACKGROUND.

St Croix national costume of about 1800, worn by a guide at The Whim. The three points in the head-dress meant that the wearer, though still married, was available and looking.

DANISH COLONIAL ARCHITECTURE IN FREDERIKSTED: A MIX OF CLASSICAL AND GINGERBREAD STYLES.

WESTEND SALT POND.

THE 18TH-CENTURY WINDMILL TOWER AT ANNABERG, THE FORMER DANISH SUGAR PLANTATION ON THE NORTH COAST. A CHARACTERISTIC FEATURE OF STONE BUILDINGS ON ST JOHN, PARTICULARLY NOTICEABLE HERE, IS THE USE OF CORAL BLOCKS AROUND DOOR AND WINDOW OPENINGS.

Cruz Bay harbour.

TWO OF THE MAGNIFICENT BEACHES ON THE ISLAND'S NORTH COAST:
Right:
CANEEL BAY.
Below:
HAWKSNEST BAY.

British

Virgin Islands

Tortola

Road Town harbour.

GINGERBREAD ARCHITECTURE IN ROAD TOWN.

CANE GARDEN BAY.

Yachts racing in the annual British Virgin Islands Spring Regatta, held off Road Town, the major sailing centre in this part of the Caribbean.

NSET OFF THE WEST SIDE OF TORTOLA,
OKING TOWARDS JOST VAN DYKE ISLAND.

BELMONT SALT POND.

SMUGGLERS' COVE BEACH.

GIORGIO HO

At the Virgin Gorda Easter Festival, held annually in Spanish Town. Mainly a family occasion for local people, it has a more relaxed and friendly atmosphere than some of the better-known carnivals.

SPRING BAY.

THE PATH TO LITTLE TRUNK BAY.

Virgin Gorda Baths. The massive granite boulders of Virgin Gorda, seen on these two pages, first appeared about 70 million years ago. Their strange shapes and cavities were formed some 50 million years later when faulting and uplifting of the sea floor occurred.

DUTCH ISLANDS

ST MAARTEN

PHILIPSBURG HARBOUR SEEN FROM POINT BLANCHE, BACKED BY THE GREAT SALT POND WHICH WAS THE ISLAND'S MAIN SOURCE OF INCOME UNTIL ABOUT 1950.

Sea shells for sale on the pier at Philipsburg. The shells are harvested locally by this family, who live and work from a small yacht.

THE HARBOUR AT OYSTER POND, ON THE EAST COAST.

AN INFORMAL CRAFT MARKET IS HELD REGULARLY ON THE PHILIPSBURG PIER.

THE OLD STREET SHOPPING CENTRE IN PHILIPSBURG.

A HOUSE IN GRAND CASE IN THE FRENCH HALF OF THE ISLAND.

A STREET SCENE (RIGHT) AND THE WESLEYAN CHAPEL (ABOVE) IN BOTTOM.

UITE DIFFERENT FROM ANY OF THE OTHER ISLANDS,
BA IS THE TIP OF AN EXTINCT VOLCANO RISING OUT OF
IE SEA. LONG THOUGHT UNINHABITABLE, ITS POPULATION
STILL ONLY ABOUT 1000, DIVIDED BETWEEN THREE
LLAGES WHICH HAVE RETAINED THEIR DISTINCTIVELY
UTCH CHARACTER AND CLEANLINESS. THE PRINCIPAL
TTLEMENT, BOTTOM, IS SITUATED AT THE LOWER END OF
IE ISLAND'S ONLY ROAD, ALTHOUGH THE NAME IS DERIVED
OM THE DUTCH WORD *BOTTE*, MEANING BOWL.

A TYPICAL HOUSE IN WINDWARDSIDE.

WINDWARDSIDE, NEAR THE TOP OF THE MOUNTAIN.

A HAND SUGAR MILL, STILL IN USE TODAY.

MARGUERITE HASSELL WORKING ON ONE OF HER TRADITIONAL LACE DESIGNS. HER OTHER SPECIALITY IS BREWING SABA SPICE, A POTENT LOCAL LIQUEUR.

Frigate Bay resort area with a catamaran regatta in progress.

A distinctive feature of St Kitts is the number of historic stone buildings which survive, as here at the Fort on Brimstone Hill, built by the British in the 18th century during their struggle with the French for possession of the island.

Painting Caribelle Batik material at Romney Manor.

Two stages in the production of cane sugar, still the island's main industry:

Above:

After the cane has been ground into small pieces, water is introduced to wash the juice out of it.

Right:

Molasses, the other end product, being extracted from the juice.

AN INFORMAL SUNDAY SCHOOL NEAR ST PAUL'S.

NEVIS

MOUNT NEVIS AND THE NATIONAL FLAG FROM THE GARDEN OF NISBET PLANTATION INN.

AN EARLY STAGE IN NELSON'S RELATIONSHIP WITH EMMA HAMILTON. THIS PAINTING IN THE NELSON MUSEUM NEAR FIG TREE, DATING FROM ABOUT 1795 AND TAKEN FROM THE BACK OF A SICILIAN CART, SHOWS HER DANCING BEFORE HIM AT THE COURT IN NAPLES.

ST JOHN'S CHURCH, FIG TREE, WHERE NELSON MARRIED THE WIDOW FANNY NISBET IN 1787.

Pinney's Beach at the new Four Seasons Hotel.

ENGLISH AND FALMOUTH HARBOURS SEEN FROM FORT SHIRLEY.

ANTIGUA IS THE SAILING CAPITAL OF THE CARIBBEAN. ON BOARD HUGH BAILEY'S YACHT, *HUGO*, IN A CLUB RACE OFF FALMOUTH.

Antigua is sometimes said to have a beach for every day of the year. This one is at Half Moon Bay on the southeast coast.

DARKWOOD BEACH ON THE SOUTHWEST COAST.

FISHING IN THE LAGOON BEHIND DARKWOOD BEACH, WITH THE MOUNTAINS OF THE RAIN FOREST IN THE BACKGROUND.

ST JOHN'S
Above:
IN REDCLIFFE STREET.
Left:
REDCLIFFE QUAY.

The ruins of the 18th-century Mast House in the grounds of Admiral's Inn at English Harbour.

MARTINIQUE

ON THE PIER AT ANSE D'ARLETS.

OUTSIDE A RESTAURANT IN ST ANNE.

HIBISCUS IN BALATA TROPICAL BOTANICAL PARK.

FISHERMEN PREPARING NETS AT ANSE D'ARLETS.

A BOAT SHED ON A SMALL ISLAND OFF LE MARIN.

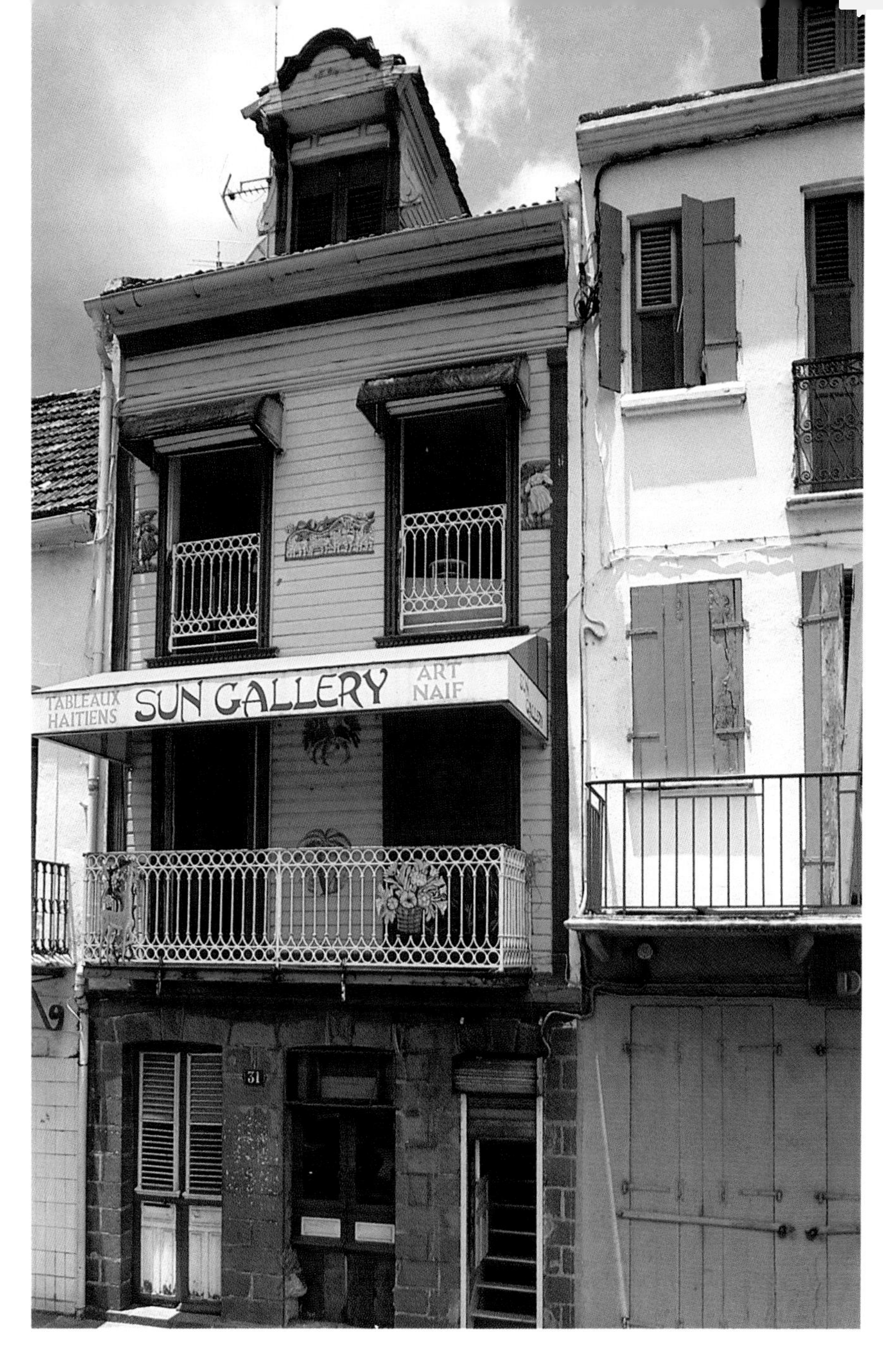

THE PICTURE GALLERY IN RUE BLENAC, FORT DE FRANCE.

In the market at Vauclin.

COCK-FIGHTING IS STILL LEGAL — AND FLOURISHING AS A BETTING MEDIUM — ON THE ISLAND.

WALL PAINTING OUTSIDE A BAR IN POINTE-À-PITRE.

A Seventh Day Adventist service on the beach at St Anne — the Minister leads hymn singing.

Baptism for a Seventh Day Adventist involves total immersion.

FOUNTAIN IN THE MARKET SQUARE AT POINTE-A-PITRE.

A SHOP IN BASSE-TERRE.

PUTTO OUTSIDE A WINDOW IN BASSE-TERRE.

LOCALLY MADE WEDDING CAKES IN A SHOP AT POINTE-NOIR.

IN THE MARCHE A MAN REO, POINTE-À-PITRE.

FAMILY PICNICKING NEAR CASCADE AUX ECREVISSES, IN THE BASSE-TERRE FOREST.

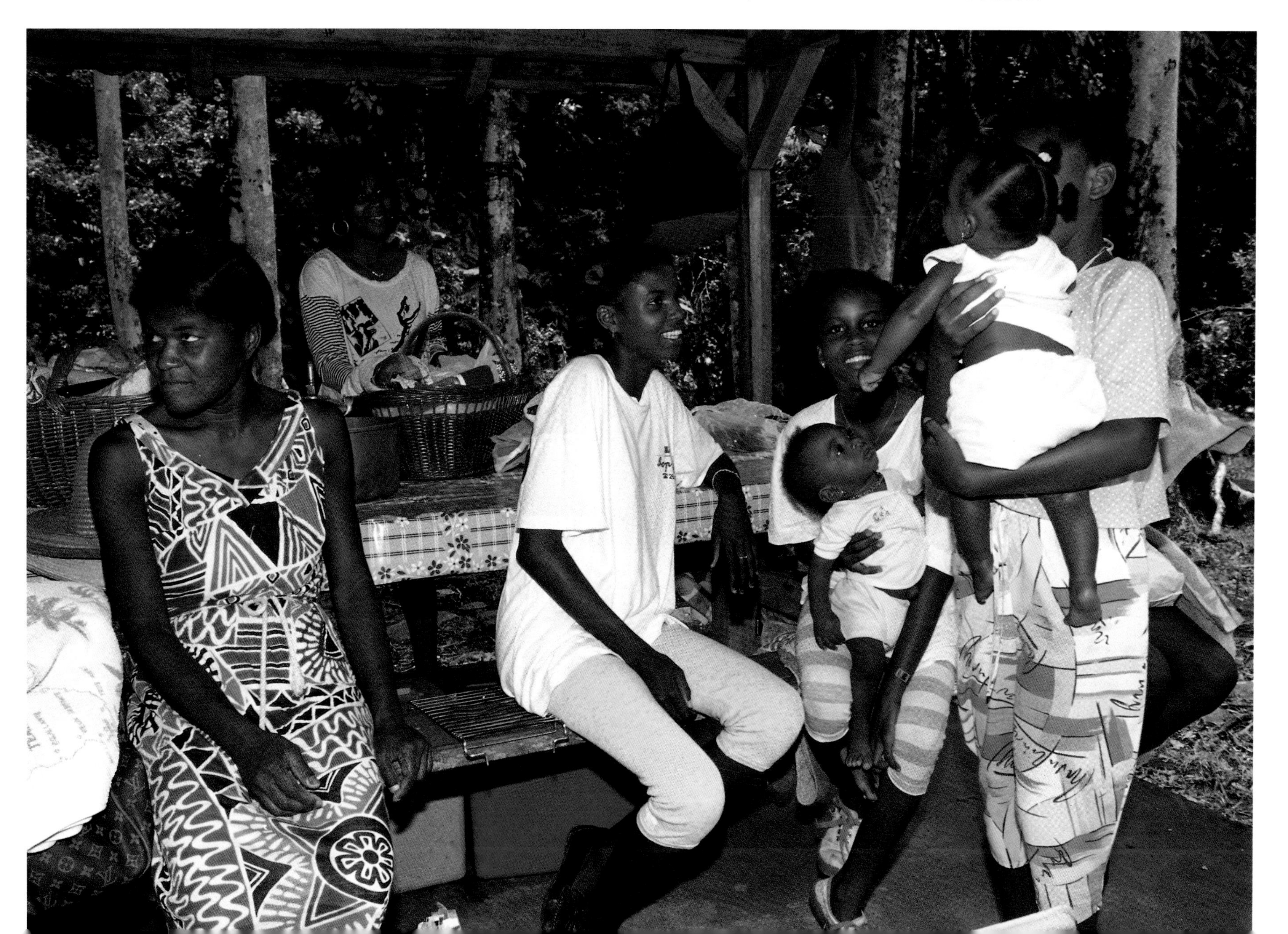

HOBIE CAT 16

POINTE DES CHÂTEAUX.

N THE BEACH NEAR CALLINAGO
OTEL.

DOMINICA

DOMINICAN NATIONAL COSTUME, PROBABLY DATING FROM THE 18TH CENTURY. THE SINGLE POINT ON THE OLDER GIRL'S HEAD-DRESS MEANT 'MY HEART IS FREE'.

FISHERMAN MENDING NETS NEAR ROSEAU.

The Emerald Pool with waterfall, in Morne Piton National Park.

Wotton Waven Sulphur Springs.

THE CHIEF OF THE CARIB INDIAN RESERVATION. ELECTED WHEN ONLY 21 AND STILL A YOUNG MAN, HIS OFFICE COMBINES THE FUNCTIONS OF A PRESIDENT AND A PRIME MINISTER. THE MACE WAS DONATED BY THE ENGLISH CROWN IN 1905.

A traditional Indian hut in the Carib Reservation.

An Indian canoe under construction. At this stage it is being widened by the pressure of stones and water, prior to firing.

THE INTERIOR OF THE 19TH-CENTURY CHURCH AT SOUFRIÈRE, WITH MURALS BY LENNOX HONYCHURCH.

OSEAU.

Castries Harbour from Morne Fortune.

In the market at Castries.

THE MARQUIS COCONUT AND BANANA PLANTATION ON THE EAST COAST.

Right:

DE-FLOWERING BANANAS BEFORE PICKING.

Below:

THE OVERSEER, VINCENT BISCETTE, AND AN ASSISTANT SPLITTING COCONUTS BEFORE PUTTING THEM IN THE OVEN.

THE PLANTATION, ESTABLISHED IN TH
18TH CENTURY, OCCUPIES A FERTIL
RIVER VALLEY STRETCHING TO THE SE

Petit Piton from Dasheene Resort Hotel

ie Pitons. The pyramidal cones of
va were formed by a volcanic
uption about 35 million years ago.

The boiling sulphur springs at Soufrière.
The low-lying volcano here has not erupted
for thousands of years, but still emits hot
vapours and gasses.

Cathy Osman, a self-employed potter of Choiseul who turns pots by hand without a wheel, finishing a charcoal container.

Making a bamboo basket, at the Choiseul Arts and Crafts Centre.

MARIGOT BAY.

ON THE BEACH AT THE WEST-COAST FISHING VILLAGE OF ANSE LA RAYE.

ST NICHOLAS' ABBEY, BUILT ABOUT 1655 AND THOUGHT TO BE ONE OF ONLY THREE JACOBEAN PLANTATION GREAT HOUSES LEFT STANDING IN THE WESTERN HEMISPHERE.

SALLY THOMAS, CO-OWNER OF SUNBURY, ARRANGING FLOWERS IN THE DRAWING ROOM.

SUNBURY PLANTATION HOUSE, LIKE ST NICHOLAS' ABBEY, DATES FROM THE 17TH CENTURY AND IS STILL A LIVED-IN HOME — THE ONLY GREAT HOUSE ON THE ISLAND WHICH OFFERS ITS VISITORS ACCESS TO THE PRIVATE ROOMS.

View over Scotland District, in t
north of the island, from Farley Hi

This massive stone lion was carved by a British officer in 1868. The Gun Hill signal station, in the background, was one of a chain of stations used by the British forces to pass information round the island.

One of the Barbados Garrison's unique collection of iron cannon, dating back to 1670, with the Savannah Club building in the background.

ALLELUIA
Though I speak with the tongues of men and of Angels, and have not Charity, I am become as a sounding brass and or a tinkling cymbal.
SONS OF GOD APOSTOLIC
SPIRITUAL BAPTIST INC.
RT. REVD. BISHOP GRANVILLE WILLIAMS
O.H.P.
SUNDAY SCHOOL - 9.30 A.M.
SUNDAY WORSHIP-3.00 P.M.
THURSDAY -7.00 P.M.
BAPTISMS: WEDDINGS
CHRISTENINGS: FUNERALS
POINTMENT
JERUSALEM APOSTOLIC CATHEDRAL
Choose you This Day whom you will serve.

ONE OF THE ISLAND'S NUMEROUS RELIGIOUS SECTS, THE TIE-HEADS, BASED AT JERUSALEM APOSTOLIC CATHEDRAL, EALING GROVE, CHRIST CHURCH.
Left: BEFORE A SERVICE

A WOMAN BRINGS HER CHILD FOR BAPTISM.

Above and below:
MEMBERS OF THE CONGREGATION AT PRAYER AND WORSHIP.

A STEEL BAND REHEARSAL BY THE STUDENTS OF GARRISON SECONDARY SCHOOL, BRIDGETOWN.

EACH NEAR SPEIGHTSTOWN.

A Barbados green monkey in the Barbados Wildlife Reserve, near Farley Hill.

Stalactites and stalagmites in on
of the coral limestone caverns a
Harrison's Cave

ST VINCENT

THE CAPITAL'S GEORGIAN ORIGINS ARE EVIDENT IN THE BOTANICAL GARDENS, ONE OF THE OLDEST IN THE WESTERN HEMISPHERE.

THE PURE CLASSICAL STYLE OF THE 18TH-CENTURY ST GEORGE'S CATHEDRAL IN KINGSTOWN.

The cannonball tree flower in the Botanical Gardens.

A collage made by a local artist, Kendal Charles, from the dried bark and leaves of banana trees, without any added colouring (Banana Art Gallery, Kingstown).

IN KINGSTOWN MARKET.

LAYOU, A WEST-COAST FISHING VILLAGE.

[illegible] VINCENT FROM YOUNG ISLAND.

FISHING BOATS AT PETIT BORDEL. THE BEACH IS OF BLACK (VOLCANIC) SAND.

CUTTING BANANAS.

A BANANA PLANTATION IN THE MESOPOTAMIA DISTRICT.

Carriacou and its Neighbours

Tyrrell Bay, Carriacou

FISHERMAN WITH LIVE LOBSTERS,
PETIT ST VINCENT.

A TRADITIONAL FISHING BOAT UNDER
CONSTRUCTION, PETIT MARTINIQUE.

ST GEORGE'S HARBOUR.

SORTING THE CATCH AT GOOYAVE.

FISHERMEN PULLING THE SEINE (A GIANT NET) NEAR GOUYAVE ON THE WEST COAST.

RAIN FOREST AND MOUNTAINS IN THE INTERIOR.

HELICONIA IN BAY GARDENS, NEAR ST GEORGE'S.

PRE-COLUMBIAN STONE CARVING ON A BEACH NEAR VICTORIA.

ST GEORGE'S MARKET ON SATURDAY MORNING.

RIPE NUTMEGS, THE ISLAND'S STAPLE CROP, READY FOR PICKING.

GRADING MACE AT THE NUTMEG RECEIVING STATION IN GOUYAVE.

NUTMEG BEING SORTED FROM MACE AT DOUGALDSTOWN ESTATE.

GRAND ETANG, A LAKE IN A VOLCANIC CRATER IN THE CENTRE OF THE ISLAND.

Concorde Falls.

ST GEORGE'S FROM THE GRANDE ANSE AREA.

SHERMEN RETURNING TO LEVERA
EACH, WITH SUGAR LOAF ISLAND IN
HE BACKGROUND.

THE KIDDIES' CARNIVAL, HELD ON THE SATURDAY BEFORE THE MAIN EVENT, IS NO LESS SPECTACULAR.

IN THE MAIN CARNIVAL PROCESSION.

One of the winners in the Calypso Singers' competition at the carnival — Denyse Plummer.

Another carnival costume.

Supporting acolytes on sta
during the calypso competitio

DETAIL OF ONE OF THE 'MAGNIFICENT SEVEN' VICTORIAN MANSIONS IN PORT OF SPAIN — THE SO-CALLED FRENCH CHÂTEAU.

TRINIDAD HAS A STRONG INDIAN COMMUNITY: VENDORS AT CHAGUANAS MARKET.

THE NORTHERN RAIN FOREST A
MOUNTAINS, FROM THE ASA WRIG
NATURAL HISTORY CENTR

CHARLOTTESVILLE — A TYPICAL TOBAGO FISHING VILLAGE.

BACOLET BAY — THE DARK SAND OF THE SOUTH COAST.

CASTARA BAY.

ON THE BEACH AT CHARLOTTESVILLE.